Rock Painting

Carrie Sharp

Even in their natural state, rocks are fascinating to kids. Imagine how irresistible they will be when painted with colorful artwork. Whether you paint just one or a set to tell a story, these rocks will be treasured.

LEISURE ARTS, INC. • Maumelle, Arkansas

PAINTING AMAZING DESIGNS ON ROCKS

Painting on rocks goes back to the age of cave dwellers when people told stories, preserved memories, and added beauty to their lives by decorating the rock walls of their caves.

Rock painting today takes on a whole new perspective with bright paint colors and fun designs. Even though we no longer need to communicate through painting on rocks, we can still add beauty to our lives and express our creativity with decorated rocks.

FINDING ROCKS

So, which comes first, the design or the rock? Both! Sometimes you have a design in mind and need to search for just the right rock. Other times you find an interesting rock that inspires you to come up with a design to compliment its shape.

Whether you call them rocks, stones, or pebbles, searching for the perfect rock can be a fun adventure. But first, you have to know where to look. It could be as simple as your own backyard or the local park.

Other places include beaches, streams, and riverbeds. Moving water continuously washing over rocks smooths and textures the surface to make the perfect canvas.

If you don't have access to natural areas for gathering rocks, many craft stores, plant nurseries, and even home improvement stores carry a selection of different rocks that may be suitable for your project.

Size
The average size used in this book is about 2" x 3" for oval rocks and about a 3" diameter for round ones.

Being flexible about the size can bring interesting results, too. You may have in mind to turn a medium size rock into a ladybug, but all you can find are smaller rocks. Why not go with it and paint an army of ladybugs! Display some on a windowsill or tuck a few in a flowerpot.

Shape
Our designs work well on slightly flat, oval and round shapes, like the rocks pictured.

Look at your chosen design; can you see it being painted on a different shape? Maybe a rock with flat end would allow a monster to stand upright. A triangular shape might lend itself to becoming a leaf.

Surface
Look for rocks with a smooth surface. Texture on the surface can add interest, but avoid bumps or jagged edges.

PREPARING ROCKS

A brushing with a stiff natural bristle brush to remove any loose dirt, a good washing with warm water and a thorough drying are all you need to do to prepare your rocks. If your rocks are particularly dirty, add a little liquid soap to the wash water and rinse with clean water.

PAINTING ROCKS

Supplies

Acrylic paint – look for a variety pack with lots of colors or if you enjoy mixing your own, just get a few basic colors.

Brushes – the ones we used most often include a 10/0 liner brush, #1 round brush, #6 round brush.

Toothpicks – used to make very small dots. Just dip the end in paint and apply to the surface.

Sealer – a final coat of waterproof clear acrylic sealer will protect the paint. Choose from glossy for bright, whimsical designs or matte for a more natural look.

Chalk pencil – to draw your design before painting, if desired. Chalk brushes away easily to allow design changes.

Fine-point permanent marker – for adding very fine details.

Plastic cup or glass – fill with water for cleaning brushes.

Small foam or plastic plates – use for mixing colors or just to hold paint.

Paper towels – always handy for spills and cleanup.

How To Basics

Always allow paint to dry between colors.

Thoroughly clean brushes when changing colors

Unless the natural color of the rock will be your background, always apply a basecoat of white paint to the entire surface of the rock. Paint one side, allow to dry and paint the other side.

Paint the entire rock with your background color.

Use white paint and a liner brush to "draw" the outline of the larger areas of the design. If desired, you can use a white chalk pencil to draw the outline then; paint over the drawn lines with white.

Fill in the drawn outline with white paint to provide an even base for darker colors.

When adding the colors over the base, work from the background up, ending with the areas that appear the closest to you.

BUGS

Whimsical butterflies, bees, grasshoppers, and ladybugs appeal to both children and the inner child in us.

Tucked into the soil of a potted plant or scattered in a flower bed, these colorful bugs will brighten your garden (and they won't nibble on your plants)!

LET'S GET STARTED!

SHOPPING LIST

- ☐ assorted oval and round smooth rocks
- ☐ acrylic paint in a variety of colors
- ☐ clear acrylic sealer
- ☐ paintbrushes:
  - 10/0 liner brush
  - #1 round brush
  - #6 round brush
- ☐ toothpicks
- ☐ black fine-point permanent marker (optional)

LADYBUG

THE STEPS

1 Choose a smooth round or oval rock. Wash the rock with warm water and dry.

2 Paint a basecoat of white on one side of the rock; allow to dry. Paint the remaining side.

3 Paint the rock green. Using white paint and a liner brush, paint a circle body, oval wings, and a half-circle head.

4 Using a round brush and following the outline, fill in the body, head, and wings with white paint.

5 Paint the head and wings red. It may take two coats so be sure to allow the paint to dry between coats.

6 Use a liner brush and black paint to outline the wings and head.
Tip: A fine-point black permanent marker can be used to draw the outline.

7 Paint the body black. It may take two coats so be sure to allow the paint to dry between coats.

8 Paint black spots on the wings, eyes, and antennae. Paint a white line for the mouth and small white dot highlights on the eyes.

PAINT A DIFFERENT BUG!

To fill your garden with a variety of these delightful insects, simply follow the basic steps (above). Turn the page to see close up photos of the rest of the collection and painting tips for creating each design.

MORE BUGS

Light brown paint provides the base of the leaf. Medium brown veins and shading with dark brown adds detail. Finish the leaf with a sprinkling of green to make it the perfect resting place for a bright red ladybug.

Brightly colored flowers attract equally colorful butterflies. Begin with the flower petals then add the flower center. Paint black butterfly body and outline for the wings. Paint the inside of the wings. Make the dots on the wings and flower center using a brush handle dipped in paint.

This colorful little guy will have you humming, "Don't Worry, Bee Happy" when you add him to your bug collection.

An almost perfectly round rock in bright purple calls for an equally bold butterfly. Keep it simple with a limited color palette of medium blue, dark blue, black, and white.

Our vivacious grasshopper looks like he is about to jump at any moment. See how just a few curved detail lines in black and white gives the illusion of movement.

SEA CREATURES

Whether you want to create a lasting memory of your trip to the ocean, teach a child about aquatic life, or you just love anything beachy, this sea creatures collection including, Starfish, Scallops, Crab, and Fish is sure to please.

Display your collection in a glass bowl or small fish tank. You could even tuck one or two into the rocks at the bottom of your aquarium.

LET'S GET STARTED!

SHOPPING LIST

- ☐ assorted oval and round smooth rocks
- ☐ acrylic paint in a variety of colors
- ☐ clear acrylic sealer
- ☐ paintbrushes:
  - 10/0 liner brush
  - #1 round brush
  - #6 round brush
- ☐ toothpicks
- ☐ black fine-point permanent marker (optional)

STARFISH

THE STEPS

1 Choose a smooth round or oval rock. Wash the rock with warm water and dry.

2 Paint a basecoat of white on one side of the rock; allow to dry. Paint the remaining side.

3 Paint the rock aqua. Using white paint and a liner brush, paint five legs to form the outline of the starfish.

4 Using a round brush and following the outline, fill in the starfish with white paint.

5 Paint over the white with coral. It may take two coats so be sure to allow paint to dry between coats.

6 Paint two blue eyes. Use a brush handle dipped in orange paint to make dots on the legs. When dry, use a smaller brush handle to make yellow dots on top of the orange ones.

7 Use a liner brush and black paint to outline the body and add black pupils to the eyes.

8 Use brush handles dipped in white, coral, yellow, and black to make dots under the starfish. Use toothpicks dipped in the different colors to make the tiny dots.

PAINT A DIFFERENT SEA CREATURE!

To paint more of these marine dwellers simply follow the basic steps (above). Turn the page to see close up photos of the rest of the collection and painting tips for creating each design.

MORE CREATURES FROM THE SEA

Just blowing bubbles and swimming along, this fish doesn't have a care in the world. Paint the body yellow then add black stripes and a white eye. Use black for outlining and adding details. For the bubbles, paint light blue circles with white highlights.

Big blue eyes and lots of details bring this crab to life. Start by painting a red body, add 6 legs, 2 claws and 2 eyes. Outline with black then add black and white detail lines. For the sand, make different size dots by using brush handles and toothpicks dipped in paint.

Look at this fish smile as he happily explores a seaweed forest on the ocean floor! Paint the body orange with white stripes. For the bubbles, paint light blue circles with white highlights. Paint assorted colors of seaweed and add dots with a toothpick dipped in white paint.

This pretty blue scallop is washed with white to give it dimension. Just add a few drops of water to a very small amount of white paint; mix well. Lightly brush the shell with the thinned paint. When dry, add outlines and details in bright pink. For the sand, make different size dots by using brush handles and toothpicks dipped in bright pink, white and tan paint.

STORY

There is a story waiting to be told with this fun collection of critters, playground equipment, and trees. Will Miss Kitty and Mr. Doggie fly a kite, climb a tree, or take turns on the slide?

It's up to you to create a plot. Where will your story take you?

LET'S GET STARTED!

SHOPPING LIST

- ☐ assorted oval and round smooth rocks
- ☐ acrylic paint in a variety of colors
- ☐ clear acrylic sealer
- ☐ paintbrushes:
  - 10/0 liner brush
  - #1 round brush
  - #6 round brush
- ☐ toothpicks
- ☐ black fine-point permanent marker (optional)

MISS KITTY

THE STEPS

1 Choose a smooth round or oval rock. Wash the rock with warm water and dry.

2 Paint a basecoat of white on one side of the rock; allow to dry. Paint the remaining side.

3 Paint the rock green. Using white paint and a liner brush, paint the outline of the cat's head and tail.

4 Using a round brush and following the outline, fill in the head and tail with white paint.

5 Leaving the inside of the ears and the neck unpainted, use a small round brush to paint the head and tail stripes pink.

6 Paint the inside of the ears, tail stripes and the neck orange.

7 Paint white ovals for the eyes. Paint a black heart-shaped nose and a red tongue and collar. Use a liner brush to outline around the eyes and tongue with black.

8 With the liner brush and black paint, outline the head and tail. Add details like whiskers, eyebrows and a chin. Use orange and white to add highlights to the face and eyes.

PAINT A DIFFERENT PLAYGROUND PAL!

To paint more of these playground pals, simply follow the basic steps (above). Turn the page to see close up photos of the rest of the collection and painting tips for creating each design.

MORE PLAYGROUND PALS

Even though he is painted blue, Mr Doggie sports a happy face! Toothpicks dipped in paint make it easy to add spots to his nose.

Not only does this smiling kite have a tail, she has arms! No wonder she can soar so high!

Falling leaves reveal a web of branches. To create the wood look start with a light brown and add streaks of darker brown.

Flying high in a sky of light blue, this bright orange and green kite has a purple tail and orange bows.

The summer tree, painted with several shades of green provides shade for the playground.

Every playground needs a slide! Brush handles and toothpicks dipped in paint add texture to the sand below.

His glow is so bright that even the sun has to wear shades as he shines over the swing set. See the fall tree, left, to create the wood look.

SUCCULENTS

It's no wonder that succulents are trendy. They are easy to grow, colorful and come in a large variety of sizes.

What's even lower maintainence than real succulents are ones painted on rocks. No watering required and you'll never prick your finger!

For an eye-catching display, fill a terra cotta pot with gravel and top with painted rocks.

LET'S GET STARTED!

SHOPPING LIST

- ☐ assorted oval and round smooth rocks
- ☐ acrylic paint in a variety of colors
- ☐ clear acrylic sealer
- ☐ paintbrushes:
  - 10/0 liner brush
  - #1 round brush
  - #6 round brush
- ☐ toothpicks
- ☐ black fine-point permanent marker (optional)

CACTUS

THE STEPS

1 Choose a smooth round or oval rock. Wash the rock with warm water and dry.

2 Paint a basecoat of white on one side of the rock; allow to dry. Paint the remaining side.

3 Paint the rock purple. Using white paint and a round brush and leaving the bloom center unpainted, paint the outline of the cactus and bloom.

4 Using a round brush and following the outline, fill in the cactus body with olive green paint. Using a liner brush, outline the cactus segments with light blue.

5 Use a liner brush to paint the cactus spines dark green.

6 Paint the lighter spines yellow.

7 Leaving the center purple, paint the bloom petals red and yellow.

8 With the liner brush and black paint, outline the cactus and bloom. Use a toothpick dipped into white paint to make the tiny dots.

PAINT A DIFFERENT SUCCULENT!

To paint more of the succulents, simply follow the basic steps (above). Turn the page to see close up photos of the rest of the collection and painting tips for creating each design.

MORE SUCCULENTS

Paint the leaves of this Aloe plant with alternating medium and light olive green. Add pebbles around the base by first painting with light brown then adding darker brown shading for dimension. Toothpicks dipped in paint were used to make the scattered white and pink dots.

Keep it natural when you paint this version of a Saguaro cactus on a tan background using olive green for the plant and brown and green for the highlights and details.

You might want to try a spicier version of a Saguaro cactus painted in bright turquoise on a bold orange background. Outline the cactus in black and add yellow details.

One of the most popular cacti for growing in pots, this Echinocereus plant is painted light green and boasts colorful pink and orange blooms. The spines and other highlights are painted with white, yellow, and a darker shade of green. A toothpick dipped in white was used to make the flower center dots.

MONSTERS

There is nothing scary about this delightful group of friendly monsters. With their happy colors, bright eyes and big smiles, these guys are sure to bring a giggle or two to your favorite child.

LET'S GET STARTED!

SHOPPING LIST

- ☐ assorted oval and round smooth rocks
- ☐ acrylic paint in a variety of colors
- ☐ clear acrylic sealer
- ☐ paintbrushes:
  - 10/0 liner brush
  - #1 round brush
  - #6 round brush
- ☐ toothpicks
- ☐ black fine-point permanent marker (optional)

ALIEN

THE STEPS

1 Choose a smooth round or oval rock. Wash the rock with warm water and dry.

2 Paint a basecoat of white on one side of the rock; allow to dry. Paint the remaining side.

3 Paint the rock orange. Using white paint and a liner brush, paint the outline of a circle body and leg.

4 Using a round brush and following the outline, fill in the body with yellow. Paint the center and shoe black.

5 Paint white stripes on the yellow body area and red stripes on the leg.

6 Paint a white "creature" in the black body area. Paint blue stripes on the yellow body area. Paint a purple stripe on the leg.

7 Paint the creature's body purple. Outline the creature in red and paint the tentacles red.

8 With the liner brush and white paint, add the triangular details to the lower body; outline with black paint. With the liner brush and black paint, outline the body, leg, and creature's body.

PAINT A DIFFERENT MONSTER!

To paint more of the monsters, simply follow the basic steps (above). Turn the page to see close up photos of the rest of the collection and painting tips for creating each design.

MORE MONSTERS

Green, blue, and red are the perfect colors for a monster painted on a teal base. Spike his hair in red and trim it with green. Add blue and yellow feet that look like wheels for this dude on the go!

Start off with a light blue rock and paint on an orange and red monster. Give her some green seaweed-like hair and pointy teeth. Add blue and green dots and highlights to the eyes to complete her look.

Bright red is the base for this one-eyed creeper. Orange and blue dotted spiky hair, a big blue rimmed eye and a happy red smile all complement the olive green body. Add white highlights to the eye for extra spark.

Too pretty to be a monster, this little gal has all four eyes on you! Paint a rock purple and make the multi-petal flower pink and yellow with blue dots. Two-tone green leaves and black shoes complete her outfit. Don't forget her long eyelashes!

A blue monster with swirly hair, striped socks, and a big grin gives you the giggles. Having one eye much larger than the other adds to the fun!

MEET CARRIE SHARP

A fan of all types of arts and crafts, Carrie Sharp enjoys creating whimsical designs that make people smile.

"What inspires me the most are children. Seeing their little faces light up when they see one of my rocks is what drives me," she says.

"What initially sparked my interest in painting rocks wasn't rocks at all. I actually started out as a children's face painter and then canvas and then rocks. My favorite projects to make are virtually any craft, from paper flowers and rag rugs to painting canvas and rocks."

One of Carrie's most rewarding activities is holding community rock hunts. "I work on this project all year. In between painting rocks for customers, I paint for the kids. In the spring and fall, I pick out several parks and hide rocks for the children to find. The next morning, I disclose the location and in a very short time the kids have found them all."

"When the children find the rocks, they post on social media and show their treasures. The countless thank-yous and smiles from the parents and children make it all worth it!"

Most of all, Carrie enjoys spending Family Day every Sunday with her husband of 28 years, three children, and two granddaughters.

Production Team: Technical Writer – Jean Lewis; Technical Associate – Mary Sullivan Hutcheson; Editorial Writer – Susan Frantz Wiles; Senior Graphic Artist – Lora Puls; Photographer – Marcus Boyce.

Made in U.S.A.